# Contents

# Meet Our W...

D1113264

**Joy A. Lawler**

Joy has a bachelor of arts in English from the University of Louisville and a master of divinity from Vanderbilt University. She is a member of the South Indiana conference, currently living in Nashville, Tennessee with her husband and two cats.

# Introduction

T his study book is a part of a series called The Bible People. This book is among the first four books we are producing at this time. They are: Bible Disciples, Bible Prophets, Bible Women, and Bible Missionaries. Hopefully, other titles will follow under other groupings.

We are aware of the cases where one person can fit in more than one grouping. A person can be a disciple as well as a missionary. A person who is a woman can also be in the grouping of prophets. Nevertheless, we are highlighting one aspect of that person's ministry in this series. It may be surprising to some readers to find out that a particular person is put in a grouping they never thought he or she belonged to. Our attempt here is to see that person from a different angle and perspective than we have generally seen in the past. But then, some persons will be in their unique ministry.

Each book at present has seven sessions on seven (or more) persons. Obviously, this is not an exhaustive list but rather a selective list of Bible people in a given category. Some of them have a large body of information and the others have very little, but we will still be able to learn valuable traits of their ministry and the impact they had in their own time and world.

In a few cases, two persons are studied in the same session because they belonged together as husband and wife (Priscilla and Aquila) or mother-in-law and daughter-in-law (Naomi and Ruth) or sisters (Mary and Martha). They jointly witnessed or created situations that impacted the history of the community in which they lived. That history has become the history of our faith and their impact has affected us as followers of the Way which God has shown us in and through Jesus Christ, who is our Savior and Lord.

We believe that these studies of the Bible People will renew our faith, strengthen our resolve to become worthy sons and daughters of God, and transform us into lighthouses and torches to give hope to the lost, and light to those in darkness.

*Statement of Purpose:* The purpose of these studies is to help us learn from the lives and ministries of some of the people in the Bible who have made a significant impact on the community of their time and who have contributed toward God's design for a God-centered life for all people, including us.

# *QuickLead®*

This QUICK information will help you effectively LEAD a session of *Bible People*, either in a class setting or for your personal study. On *Bible People* pages look for the following:

## ICONS

Six icons show you at a glance what kind of activity you are asked to do, such as reflection, group discussion, or interaction. See page 4 for more specific information about the icons.

## MAIN TEXT

The text contains the basic information about the Bible person or provides leads on where and how to discover more information on your own. You will also find open space there for writing notes from your research.

## MARGINAL NOTES

Instructions for leading the session or for your own personal study are found in the margins. Questions for reflection or discussion are here too.

For more information, read the series introduction and the other articles in this issue of *Bible People*.

*The following text appears on the sample page illustration:*

Chapter Four

## Ruth and Naomi

CHOOSE FROM AMONG THESE ACTIVITIES TO REFLECT ON HOW RUTH AND NAOMI'S STORY AFFECTS YOUR FAITH.

### Meet Ruth and Naomi
Take two minutes to recall as many details, in order, as you can of the story of Ruth and Naomi. Jot down notes in the space provided. Then take turns reconstructing the story aloud.

Discuss your answers to the questions.

### What Does the Bible Say About Ruth and Naomi?

#### Meet Ruth and Naomi
Pool information about the story of Ruth and Naomi before looking at the text.

• Do any key verses stand out?

• What memories do you share about the story of Ruth and Naomi?

### Check Your Story
Read Ruth in your Bible. Since the book is short, the whole group could read the entire story. Or, form four teams and ask each team to check one chapter.

See how well your memories served you.

### Check Your Story
Jot down notes about what happens in the story.

# *Icons*

Icons are picture/symbols that show you at a glance what you should do with different parts of the main text or learning options during a reflection or study session in the *Bible People* series. The six kinds of icons are

**Discussion**—Either the main text or a marginal note will suggest discussion questions or discussion starters.

**Group Interaction**—Either the main text or a marginal note will provide instructions for how to do a group activity that requires more interplay among group members than a discussion.

**Bible Study**—Individuals studying *Bible People* are encouraged to dig into the Bible and mine the Scriptures to learn more about the Bible person and his or her contribution to the faith. Bible study may be done in a group or on your own.

**Bible Tools**—*Bible People* uses the "discovery" method of teaching, using various Bible reference tools, such as dictionaries, commentaries, atlases, and concordances. Activities that require more than the Bible will be identified with this icon. (See pages 5-7 on "The Discovery Method" and the inside back cover for "Bible Reference Tools")

**Reflection**—Group or individual *Bible People* students will have opportunities to think over questions, information, new insights, assumptions, and learnings. On occasion, the text will provide open space for written reflections.

**Worship**—Sessions may begin or end with time for corporate or private devotions.

# The Bible Discovery Method™ of Study

We are made in the image of God, and we yearn for God. Sometimes that is where our similarities end! As unique individuals in search of a relationship with the divine, we come to the task in ways as diverse as humankind. Each of us has a particular and personal perspective on the Scriptures because of our individual experiences. Our acquaintance with the Bible is influenced by our general attitude about what the Bible is and how it is to be used, as well as by a host of other factors. Each of us learns in our own way; some by doing, others by listening, others by watching, yet others by figuring out for themselves.

## Discovering the Bible

There is no single "right" way to learn, although much published curricula and many Bible study teachers depend on a few tried methods, particularly lecture, reading from study books, and group discussion. While there is certainly value in these educational practices, a more interactive or personally invested approach often helps a lesson "stick" better. Persons remember best what they experience the most intimately.

The *Bible People* series study depends on what we are calling the "discovery" method. Rather than providing all the background information about a Bible person, we are inviting you as learners to do some of your own digging, through

- the Scriptures
- Bible commentaries
- Bible dictionaries
- Key word or topical concordances
- and other Bible reference materials.

The items selected for further study can be found in most basic Bible resources. You do not need to have a specific dictionary or commentary. Most of these reference materials may be available in your church library.

## Three Main Questions

The sessions are organized around three main questions:

● What does the Bible say about the person?
● What else would we like to know about the Bible person?
● How does what I know about the Bible person affect my life and faith?

Throughout the session you will discover what some or all of the references to each Bible person say and mean. Some information will be provided directly. Other information will come to you through your own discovery, perhaps by

● looking at maps;
● looking up key words in a concordance and then finding the appropriate passages;
● researching a specific Bible reference in a commentary;
● reading entries about key words, concepts, or persons in a Bible dictionary.

All of these activities can be done in a personal, self-study setting; most will also lend themselves to group work and discussion. The length of your study session can be adapted to the time you wish to spend in exploration.

## Answering the Questions

In some cases, the biblical information is abundant. In others, the Scriptures may mention only a few verses about that Bible person. But whether the Bible offers a little insight or a lot, there is much more to learn. With hints and suggestions about where to look and what to look for, the discovery method draws you further into the life and times of each Bible person introduced in this series. To help focus the discovery method, the three organizing questions for each session provide a direction for investigation.

**The first question, What does the Bible say about the person? delves into the Scripture text for specific references about the Bible figure.**

Some of the persons featured in this series are characters whose record in Scripture is quite brief, perhaps only a few verses. Others are much more prominent. When the biblical information is scant, you will be able to review all the references. If the Bible figure is more prominent, only a selection of representative passages are indicated. If you want to dig deeper, the Bible reference tools will help you locate more information.

Whether the biblical references are few or numerous, the Bible and other sources offer much more information than you might immediately notice.

**The second question, What else would we like to know about the Bible person? mines the less direct sources of information.**

What is the context of the action? Who are the related characters who the featured Bible person influenced or was influenced by? What are the social and economic conditions that help us understand the person and his or her situation? Where does the action take place? These and other questions expand the picture and help you see more fully into the life and times of each biblical character in these studies.

**Once the portrait has become more clear, the third question, How does what I know about this person affect my life and faith? helps you apply your new insights to your own life.**

This question is the "so what?" or the "now what?" aspect of the study that links the ancient text to our contemporary lives and issues. In answering this question, the study facilitates self-discovery and, we hope, spiritual growth and transformation.

# Bible People and Study Skills

All learners have different levels of acquaintance with the Bible and of skills to study the Bible. This article presents a few pointers for how to approach *Bible People*, depending on the level of those skills. Refer to the list on the inside back cover for a description of each of the tools mentioned.

## Beginning Skills

### Use a study Bible

- Use a good study Bible with notes, cross-referencing, and maps. Buy a new one if you need to.
- Be sure that the text is a translation that is readable and under-standable for you. *Bible People* uses the New Revised Standard Version as its primary translation.
- Take some time to learn how to "get around" in the Bible. Use the table of contents to find the books and to see what else is in there. Many Bibles have articles, charts, maps, and other information in addition to the biblical text.
- *Get Acquainted With The Bible* (Abingdon Press) is an excellent introductory resource to help you learn what is in the Bible and how to use it. (Call 1-800-672-1789 and order #140463.)

### Look over a one-volume dictionary of the Bible.

- Check to see if it contains a table of contents and/or an index.
- Read any self-promotional material that will help you understand what is contained in the dictionary.
- Then thumb through it, randomly reading any entry that catches your eye.

### Acquaint yourself with a Bible commentary, perhaps a one-volume commentary for starters.

- Choose three or four of your favorite Bible passages and look them up, noting what new insights come from an expanded view of the text.
- Peruse the table of contents to see what else is there and skim through the articles.

# Intermediate Skills

### Introduce yourself to the other study tools: concordance, atlas, other sources.

- Pick a key word from one of your favorite texts and look it up in the concordance. Is the same text in more than one passage? How is that key term used elsewhere?
- Look up a concept, such as *hospitality* or *marriage* in a topical concordance. What are the citations? How are these entries different from an alphabetical concordance?
- Check for a table of contents or an index, or flip through the pages to see what else is contained in the concordance. Read the introduction, if there is one.
- Thumb through an atlas to see what kinds of maps, graphs, charts, and other information is there.
- Look up the places mentioned from one of your favorite Bible stories. How far are they from each other? What is the terrain like? What would a traveler be likely to encounter on the route?
- Check to see if key information is provided for particular cities (like Jerusalem) or for prominent geographical features (such as Mount Horeb). If this is not in the atlas, use a Bible dictionary as well.

### Read the text, then ask questions of the text.

- Who is involved in this passage? Who do they represent?
- Who is not present? Who is not represented?
- What is going on?
- Who is the audience? What are they like?
- Who is involved with the central figure(s) of the text? What impact do the characters have on each other?
- What is the context? What is the central message?
- What did that message mean then? What relevance does it have now? now for you?
- What is not happening?
- What emotions might have been felt by the figures presenting the story, text, or action? by the audience? now by you?
- What do you notice about the story, after using several resources to gain more information, that you didn't know or notice before? What difference does that make to your faith and understanding now?

# Advanced Skills

### Dig deeper into the cultural aspects and other details.
● Use the Bible study tools to look into details that the text suggests or assumes its original readers would already understand, such as, What did it mean to be a slave or widow or head of household? What did neighboring religions do in the same situation or region? Where is the action taking place and what was the situation there? How much is something worth? How long did it take to get there and what method of travel would have been used? What was the social/economic/political climate historically?

### Use biblical-era sources in addition to the Bible and standard reference tools.
● Certain biblical passages are mentioned also in the Apocrypha or the historical context is the same. Check them out. Many Bibles include the Apocrypha, which most Orthodox religious groups (such as Roman Catholics) and some Protestant denominations (such as Episcopalians) regard as part of the canonized (or "official") Scripture.
● Look for references, concepts, and historical events in church encyclopedias, dictionaries, or historical writings. You may need an excellent public library or a theological library to obtain these texts, although most good bookstores have some biblical-era references.

### Cross-reference passages to see what is said about the same or similar situation elsewhere in the Bible.
● When an annotated Bible provides cross-references or notes that refer to other passages, look them up.
● Many passages, especially in the Gospels, are recorded more than once. Look up the same event in another biblical book to see how it differs or agrees with the other citation(s).
● Ask yourself the exploratory questions as you compare texts.
● Use a concordance to look for several instances of the same word, event, social situation, and so on in the Bible. Look up the various references to see how the Bible's treatment varies (or not) to get a composite picture or overview of an issue.

*Chapter One*

# Rahab

**CHOOSE FROM AMONG THESE ACTIVITIES TO REFLECT ON HOW RAHAB'S STORY AFFECTS YOUR FAITH.**

### *Rahab the Harlot*

 Using a Bible diction- ary, look up the word *harlot*. (Harper's Bible Dictionary [Harper and Row, 1985] has a lengthy entry.)

- What new information did you gain?
- What is your initial impression of a harlot as an agent for God's plans?

God tends to choose those whom society scorns for some of the most important work in the Bible. Look up these examples:

- Genesis 32:22-32. (Jacob, patriarch of Israel)

- Luke 2:8-20. (Shepherds were considered to be dirty, smelly, and not very smart.)

- Mark 16:1-18. (Women were not considered smart enough to be reliable witnesses.)

- Acts 9:1-22. (Saul had been slaughtering the Christians.)

# *What Does the Bible Say About Rahab?*

## Rahab the Harlot

Rahab is one of the most interesting fig- ures in the Bible. She is a woman of questionable character, and a nonbeliever to boot, and yet she was the first convert to faith in the God of Moses since the dramatic escape of the Hebrew people from Egypt. She—for some reason not given—had eyes to see and ears to hear what others did not: the Almighty God of Israel "is indeed God in heaven above and on earth below" (Joshua 2:11).

Rahab was a prostitute. There is no other way to describe her occupation, although many have tried to pretty up her charac- ter. She may have been a "sacred" prosti- tute because the Canaanite religion did offer sacred places where worshipers mated in the hope of inspiring the gods to reproductive activity. But the gist of the story seems to lead the listener to understand that she was not a sacred prostitute, but was in fact as secular as secular can be.

*Rahab the Heroine*

- Why do you think Rahab was proclaimed a heroine?
- Why do you think this story was told over and over, despite the fact that she was a prostitute?
- Does God tend to choose people of impeccable character, or those whom society scorns? Give examples of your responses.

Search the Scriptures in the text to see what else we are told about Rahab. Use commentaries on those passages for other notes or insights.

Respond to the question in the text and discuss your answers.

Matthew 1 provides the genealogy of Christ. Some names in the list are omitted, such as Ahaziah, Joash, and Amaziah (see 1 Chronicles 3:11-12). Omissions were often a part of Jewish recounting of genealogies; sometimes the act of omission had meaning, as it probably did for Matthew. He wanted to connect Jesus to the line of David in all the ways he could, so he might have put together three lists of fourteen generations, given that fourteen is the numerical value for the name David in Hebrew.

# Rahab the Heroine

Tradition suggests that Rahab became the devoted wife of Joshua after the destruction of Jericho and lived happily with her new community all her remaining days. Joshua was a charismatic leader who stepped into the shoes of Moses to lead the people during the Conquest period. Perhaps this is the folk tradition Matthew knew when he placed Rahab in the genealogy of the ancestors of Christ. How else does Scripture remember Rahab?

◆ Matthew 1:1-17 (verse 5)

◆ Hebrews 11:31

◆ James 2:25

Write down what you believe are the characteristics of a good person.

*The Great Escape*

- Why, do you think, did Rahab suddenly convert to the Hebrew faith?
- Did she perhaps do the wrong thing for the right reasons or the right thing for the wrong reasons?
- How might she have known so much about the God of the Hebrews?

There are many stories of dramatic escape through a window in the Bible.

◆ David (1 Samuel 19:12)

◆ Paul (Acts 9:25, 2 Corinthians 11:33).

*Holy War and Conquest*

We who live in the late twentieth century have a hard time getting past the violence in this story. It is evident that the Hebrews are fighting a holy war, but given our experience with terrorists in our own time, this story rings harsh on our ears. The absolute destruction of Jericho was evil, but

## The Great Escape

Rahab converted from her own Canaanite religion; indeed, she seemed to know in advance about the power of the God of the Israelites. She spoke of God, for herself and her countrymen, in reverent terms.

# *What Else Would We Like to Know About Rahab?*

## Holy War and Conquest

The people of Israel had reached the end of their forty years of wilderness wandering. It was time for them to enter the Promised Land under the leadership of Joshua.

However, gaining entry into Canaan, the

in the minds of the people at the time, it was a necessary evil. In addition, though Scripture often calls for complete destruction, sociological and archeological data seldom show such obliteration.

Notice that they kill everything in sight, even the animals, which could have been of some use to them. They believed that any remaining Palestinian influence could destroy the faith of Israel (Deuteronomy 20:10-21). But God's purpose for the people was served even by this evil. God created a new people, giving birth to a new faith.

 Divide the eight movements of the story among several small groups of participants. Ask each group to look over their passage and to report the details to the other groups.

● What happened?
● What previously overlooked details did you notice?
● What part did Rahab play?
● What is gained by each of the participants in the story?
● What is your portrait of God from this whole story?
● With which character do you most identify? Why?
● What details seem absent from the story?

Promised Land, was going to be no easy task. The people who already lived there did not think it was such a good idea for the Hebrew people to sack their cities and take their land. Joshua and the tribal leaders made plans and drew up strategies for the conquest. Follow the movement of the story.

◆ Joshua sent spies (Joshua 2:1).

◆ Rahab hid the spies and lied for them (2:2-7).

◆ Rahab spoke on behalf of her countrymen and asked for a pledge of security (2:7-14).

◆ The spies made their promise (2:17-22).

◆ The spies escaped (2:15-16, 23-24).

◆ The city was sieged (6:1-14).

◆ The city was conquered (6:15-21).

◆ The promise to Rahab was made good (6:22-25).

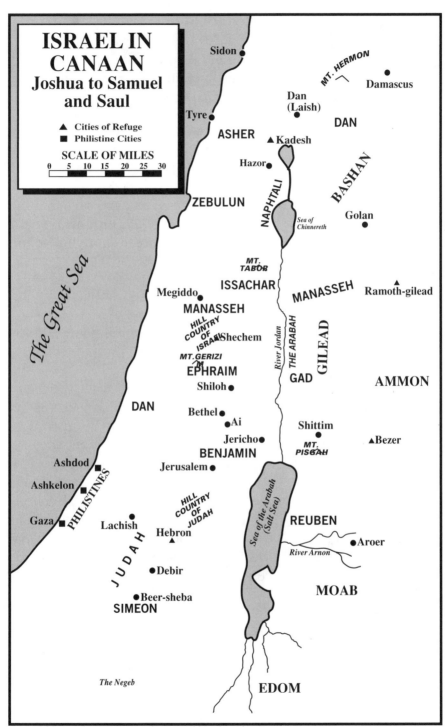

## ISRAEL IN CANAAN
### Joshua to Samuel and Saul

▲ Cities of Refuge
■ Philistine Cities

SCALE OF MILES
0  5  10  15  20  25  30

Sidon ●

MT. HERMON

Damascus ●

Dan (Laish) ●

DAN

Tyre ●

ASHER

▲ Kadesh

BASHAN

Hazor ●

ZEBULUN

NAPHTALI

Sea of Chinnereth

Golan ●

MT. TABOR

The Great Sea

ISSACHAR

MANASSEH

Ramoth-gilead ▲

Megiddo ●

MANASSEH

HILL COUNTRY OF ISRAEL

Shechem

River Jordan

THE ARABAH

GILEAD

MT. GERIZI

EPHRAIM

Shiloh ●

GAD

AMMON

DAN

Bethel ●

Ai ●

Shittim ●

Jericho ●

MT. PISGAH

▲ Bezer

BENJAMIN

Ashdod ■

Jerusalem ●

Ashkelon ■

PHILISTINES

Gaza ■

HILL COUNTRY OF JUDAH

Sea of the Arabah (Salt Sea)

REUBEN

Lachish ●

Hebron ▲

Aroer ●

River Arnon

JUDAH

● Debir

● Beer-sheba

MOAB

SIMEON

The Negeb

EDOM

From *Bible Teacher Kit,* Copyright © 1994 by Abingdon Press.

## Red Ribbon

 Look up the passages indicated in the text to find out more about the use of red items. Use commentaries for added information.

- What connections do you see with the use of a red cord for Rahab and the significance of red for the Hebrews?
- Rahab, as a Canaanite, is not likely to have known that significance, but to display the cord immediately must have drawn attention.
- What risks did Rahab take?
- What signs, symbols, or actions signify for you the ability to "turn away evil"?
- How did you become acquainted with those symbols?

The Mishnah is a collection of interpretations and elaborations on Jewish law. For more information on the red cord, see Yoma 6:2-8 in the Mishnah.

To obtain a copy of the Mishnah, check with a Jewish Orthodox congregation in your area, your local library, or a theological library

## The Red Ribbon

For us, red is sometimes associated with prostitution (as in "red light district"), but it meant something else entirely to the Hebrews. Given the opportunity the red cord gave Rahab and her family to be saved from destruction, both literally and spiritually, the meaning of the red cord may have carried a deep meaning.

◆ Red was believed to have saving power, that is, it could turn away evil. (See the red heifer ceremony in Numbers 19:1-10.)

◆ Red, or scarlet, was symbolic of honor and riches. (See Exodus 26:1 and Numbers 4:8 regarding Temple decorations and Genesis 38:27-30 on the delivery of a firstborn son.)

◆ For their services of atonement, the Hebrew priests would tie a red cord on the horns of a goat that was destined to be sacrificed as a scapegoat for atonement for the sins of the people. (This traditional belief, elaborated on in the Mishnah, is not mentioned in the Bible, although the ritual involving the scapegoat is mentioned. See Leviticus 16:20-22.)

# How Does What I Know About Rahab Affect My Life and Faith?

*Victim, Predator*

- In what ways might Rahab have been a victim in this story?
- In a modern setting, how might she be a victim?
- Rahab seemed to have a prescience, a foreknowledge of what God would do, and she arranged to save her family only. Does this make her a predator of sorts?
- When we fail to live in a way that is healthy or safe for our community, are we predatory?
- What responsibility do we have for securing the safety of the poor, the victim, the marginalized?
- If we fail in that duty, what kind of result might we find? Who might be "utterly destroyed" and by whom?

## Victim and Predator

In every age the figure of the prostitute has been a shunned and scorned person. And yet every culture has produced some form of harlot over and over again. For whatever reason a culture produces harlots, the harlot is always seen as a negative figure. The harlot would not have elicited much sympathy from the ancient culture, no matter what the circumstances that led to her choice of profession. She may be a victim, but she was also considered a predator, taking advantage of the weakness of men for her own gain.

**Marginalized, Heroic**

 Ask the group to name "harlot"-type figures in our own culture. Write these names on a chalkboard or on poster paper. Then discuss what it would be like if God chose one of these people as a hero or heroine of the Christian faith.

## Marginalized and Heroic

Even in stories of heroic "heart of gold" harlots, Rahab may have been recognized as a good person despite her choice of profession. By typical standards for her culture, she could never be a wife, and she would never be a lady.

● What might the Christian faith have to offer to some of the people who have been named?

● Do you think Christianity would be attractive to them? Why or why not?

Rahab is, beyond a doubt, a marginalized person, who probably had as much reason to hate the Canaanite rulers as anyone. The rulers routinely gained wealth by exploiting the weak, the poor, and the marginalized. We can assume that Rahab was not treated well by those in power.

It is not a coincidence that Rahab found this new religion to be attractive. After all, these Hebrews were freshly liberated from slavery; they knew what it meant to be poor, marginalized, scorned, and used. She recognized the sacred story of Israel because it was what she hoped would be her story: a deliverance by God to a new life of hope and promise. The new religion brought a sociological change along with it: they had a strong commitment to care for the poor, the widow, the orphan, the victim—this was a radical new notion of how to run a society. Maybe the Hebrews offered Rahab an opportunity to be restored to a status that she had never dared hope to reach. Though she is not your traditional role model, her story is one of blind faith, resistance to power, and hope for the future.

- Can you relate to the feeling of being outcast and scorned? If so, how has your faith helped you?

- What is the good news in Rahab's story? How does that apply to your life?

*The Power of God*

 Reflect on the questions in the text. Jot down some ideas in the space provided if you wish. Discuss your responses.

## The Power of God

Rahab recognized the power of the God of the Hebrews immediately. Perhaps she had developed a keen ability to read people and situations. She risked her life for the sake of her new faith. Maybe the chance for a new life at last was worth the risk.

- Is Rahab a negative or positive figure for you?

● What hope can you glean from this story for your own life?

● This story proves the adage, "God works in mysterious ways." How has the story of Rahab changed your view of the Almighty God of Israel?

*Worship*

 Summarize your learnings from the session and close with prayer.

*Chapter Two*

# Rebekah

CHOOSE FROM AMONG
THESE ACTIVITIES TO
REFLECT ON HOW
REBEKAH'S STORY
AFFECTS YOUR FAITH.

## What Does the Bible Say About Rebekah?

### *An Oath*

 Look up the tradition of the swearing of oaths in a Bible dictionary. Read the text and Genesis 24:1-9.

### An Oath (Genesis 24:1-9)

Rebekah was unaware of the plans being made that would ultimately involve her as part of the great lineage issuing from the covenant of God with Abraham.

- Why did Abraham take his servant's mission so seriously?
- Why does Isaac need a wife from Abraham's own people?
- Why do you think the servant devised the test that he did? What would it say about Rebekah if she offered to water his camels?

Locate on a map the cities of Ur, Haran, and Hebron. The servant returned to Aram-naharaim near the Tigris and Euphrates Rivers.

- What is the significance of each city?
- How far did the servant travel to fulfill his mission?
- How might you interpret Abraham's apparently conflicting desires: to remain among the Canaanites while insisting on a wife for Isaac from among his own kin?

### A Routine

Use a Bible dictionary to get an overview of Rebekah's life. Read the text and Scripture that introduce Rebekah to the biblical story.

### A Stranger

Research traditions of hospitality in a Bible dictionary. For more on traditions of hospitality, read Genesis 18:1-8 and Genesis 19:1-11. From these stories we get the phrase "entertaining angels unaware."

● How did Rebekah demonstrate this hospitality?

## A Routine (Genesis 24:10-14)

It was just like any other day. How was I to know how differently it would turn out? But I did not know, so I spent the day working as always. Toward evening, I went to the well to draw water as usual.

## A Stranger (24:15-27)

There was a stranger at the well who had many camels—and a lot of other men with him. He was peering at me intently, apparently studying me. His camels looked plenty thirsty. I had been carefully instructed in the customs of hospitality by my mother, and so when he asked me, I gave him a drink and offered to water his camels for him.

A look of relief, and maybe even joy, lit up his face as he ran to his pack for—can you believe this?—expensive rings and bracelets. He placed these treasures in my nose and on my arms—for watering his camels! I knew something extraordinary was happening, so I invited the stranger home for dinner and a place to sleep.

Review the Scripture and the text to introduce Laban. He seemed dazzled by all the jewelry.

- What kind of clues about the later relationship between Laban and Jacob do we get in this story?
- Speculate as to why Laban is presented as the man of the house who can negotiate for Rebekah's hand, and not her father. Is her father feeble? Is it necessary for the later story to show Laban's shrewd personality at this point?

Read Genesis 29—31 for more on the relationship between Jacob and Laban.

Look up "Weights and measures" or "Money" in a study Bible or dictionary to get an approximate worth of the jewelry.

## A Brother (24:28-51)

To put it kindly, my brother Laban is a shrewd businessman. He hurried over to the man and told him he had everything prepared for his comfort and for the care of his camels. The man finally spoke the true nature of his errand before he would agree to eat at our table. I was shocked. This was the day I had been preparing for all my life, the day somebody would come to claim me as his wife. Laban did most of the talking, and before I knew it, I was sold off like so much property. Only when the stranger was ready to leave was I asked if I were willing to go. Actually, I could have refused, but my maids and I left with the blessing of my family.

I did like the wonderful treasures the man brought as gifts, though. Apparently I am to be married to a rich man; at least I will not have to worry about that. The next morning we left to meet my husband-to-be. It was the last time I ever saw my mother or my home.

## A Journey (24:52-61)

The trip was fairly comfortable, and the men treated me with respect. But what of my future husband? Would he be kind to me? Would he be old and feeble? Would I please him? Would we love each other? When we got near our destination, I saw a man walking toward us in the field and was told it was my husband-to-be. I quickly covered myself, as my mother had taught me, so he could not see me.

## A Husband (24:62-67)

Isaac is not so bad. He is fabulously wealthy; and perhaps a little old. The unbelievable thing is he loves me! He worships the ground I walk on. Apparently he loved his mother very much, and it has not been too long since she died. He tells me I am the only one who has brought him comfort since her death. I wish I had known the woman who raised such a tender and gentle son.

*A Prayer*

Look over the text and the Scripture.

- What kind of pressures did infertile couples face in biblical times? today?
- The people of the Bible assumed it was always the woman's fault if she were unable to conceive. How do you understand that in light of biblical culture? Is this still the case today?
- How does this story help us to understand the kind of God we serve?
- Despite their best efforts, Isaac and Rebekah could not fulfill their responsibility to the covenant promise. Have you ever felt frustration at not being able to satisfy what you feel called to do?

*Barrenness* was a common theme in the Bible. For further insight, look the word up in a Bible dictionary and see also the stories of Sarah, Hannah, the wife of Manoah, and Elizabeth (Chapter 5).

## A Prayer (25:19-21)

Isaac and I prayed mightily about my barrenness. Regardless of my fine lineage, the promise given to Abraham was in peril. You see, Isaac was the product of a miracle-birth; his mother was very old when she had him; but he was the first-born in what was supposed to be a long line of descendants to number the sand of the sea and the stars of the sky. If I could not produce any children, this covenant promise was in very big trouble. But God intervened.

Using a Bible dictionary and commentary, look up the meanings of *Jacob, Esau,* and *Israel.*

- What is the meaning and significance of these names? of the play on words of Esau's name?
- How do the names portend or play out the history of Israel?
- How is the theme of subordination related to the names of the key figures?
- What did this struggle mean? Look for instances of this struggle throughout the session.

Name instances when you felt pushed or called as a Christian to do something you did not want to do.

Give examples of historical figures or contemporaries who did what was unpopular for the sake of what they thought were God's purposes. How have these choices affected the people around them?

## A Struggle (25:22)

I am so frightened. What can it mean that these babies struggle so with each other? Is a dark power controlling the children in my womb? My women friends say it is natural to be anxious before the birth of your first child, but I think this struggling and fighting is not normal.

## An Oracle (25:23)

God has spoken to me. I did not tell Isaac what God said; it would have broken his poor heart. God said words to me that are scandalous in the world we live in: The elder child will serve the younger child. This is not the correct order of things. God will have to take charge of this situation. I am at wit's end.

*A Birth, A Deception*

 Read the Scripture and the texts. Discuss as a group why you think this story has been so popular.

- How does Rebekah's attitude about her sons contribute to the events to come?
- In what ways does this story reflect the history of Israel's struggle for land and autonomy?
- How do you feel about underdogs?

## A Birth (25:24-28)

You would never believe my boys are brothers—let alone twins—by the looks of them. Esau is strong and red and hairy; Jacob is gentle and quiet and small. They have caused a disagreement between me and Isaac for the first time in all the years we have been married. Isaac loves Esau better, but I love my sensitive, intelligent, domestic Jacob. Who could not love a boy who loves his mother like he does? I did not mean to favor one over the other, but I love Jacob more.

## A Deception (25:29-34; 27:1-29)

I know it was not right; I know I overstepped my rights as a wife. I manipulated the affections of my husband shamelessly, and with Jacob, have broken Isaac's heart after all. Isaac is old and blind, and when he needed me most, I used his infirmity against him.

I just could not forget God's oracle about how things were supposed to be between these two sons of mine. The struggle they started even before they were born has never let up, and I believe wholeheartedly that it is God's will that Jacob receive the blessing.

But I know something Isaac does not know: I know about the birthright. I know how much Esau cared about all that was rightfully his; he squandered his birthright to Jacob over a bowl of stew. Then he deliberately chose a foreign wife. Jacob had to get the blessing, even if it meant disappointing Isaac in his last days. I am sorry, Isaac. If you must curse anyone, curse me.

## A Plan (27:30—28:9)

I am afraid Esau will kill his brother. I will tell Isaac that I fear that Jacob will also marry a nonbeliever, which will jeopardize the plan God has for our people. This is a true concern of mine, and Isaac agreed. Perhaps Isaac knows deep down in his heart that it is Jacob who will carry on the promise. We are sending Jacob to the home of my brother Laban. I hope he fares well.

*A Plan*

 The passages in the Bible that discourage intermarriage have been used to justify racial prejudice. The peoples were not necessarily of different races, but of different religions. Review the text and Scripture.

● How do you feel about interreligious marriages?
● Why do you think it was so important to refrain from intermarriage in early Judaism?
● What does the deception and intrigue suggest about human nature? about our religious history?

# What Else Would We Like to Know About Rebekah?

*A Burial*

 Review the text and Scripture and discuss the question in the text.

## A Burial (49:29-33)

We are not told anything about the death and burial of Rebekah, even though we get details about the deaths of Sarah, Abraham, Ishmael, Isaac, Rachel, Leah, Jacob, and Joseph. We can assume that Rebekah was separated from most of her family: Abraham and Isaac were dead, Jacob had moved away, and she was not exactly on good terms with Esau. She was buried in the ancestral burial cave, but we do not know when or how she died.

- Is it important to know the details of a person's death? Why or why not?

*A Birthright*

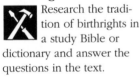 Research the tradition of birthrights in a study Bible or dictionary and answer the questions in the text.

- How was the inheritance typically divided?
- What difference would this make for the first-born and later sons?
- What impact does this custom have on the story? on what Rebekah did to manipulate the circumstances?

## A Birthright

A birthright is a powerful thing, as is a deathbed blessing. Ancient people believed that a blessing, like a curse, is like an arrow: it goes straight to the intended target, and cannot be revoked.

- Why did Rebekah take such a risk? Why do you think she was willing to take the curse on herself?

# How Does What I Know About Rebekah Affect My Life and Faith?

*A Conundrum*

Review the data you have gathered about Rebekah.

- How do her actions and attitudes parallel our lives today?
- Would you do something similar to serve God? to help your children? to influence your spouse? Why?

Answer and discuss the questions in the text.

## A Conundrum

- Why do you think Jacob was chosen by God over Esau?

- Why is Rebekah considered a heroine of the faith, and Jacob given the honor of being the father of the sanctuary of Bethel?

- How do the actors serve the purposes of God?

- Who is really in charge here? How do we know?

- Did Rebekah and Jacob really manipulate events, or were they instruments of God's plan from the beginning?

- Have you ever known anyone who was blessed, but you did not think he or she deserved it?

- God makes choices and decisions, but does not offer explanations. Is it difficult to serve such a God? Why or why not?

- How has the study of Rebekah affected your faith?

*Worship*

Review your learnings from the session and close with prayer.

## Chapter Three

# Bathsheba

**CHOOSE FROM AMONG THESE ACTIVITIES TO REFLECT ON HOW BATHSHEBA'S STORY AFFECTS YOUR FAITH.**

***The Company We Keep***

 Use a Bible dictionary to get an overview of David's life.

Look up the word *adultery* in a Bible dictionary.

- What constituted adultery in ancient times?
- Did David break the law? Did Bathsheba?
- What would have been the consequences for David if the secret had become known? for Bathsheba?

 Discuss your responses to the writing assignment in the text.

## *What Does the Bible Say About Bathsheba?*

### The Company We Keep

Bathsheba's is a story of passion—not necessarily her passion, but the passions of the men around her. There is adultery, murder, war, and political intrigue happening in her story. To know Bathsheba is to know the men who shaped her life. We hear very little from Bathsheba herself—she speaks only three times—but she was a critical figure in the life of David, the great king of Israel.

Write what you know about David.

Write what you know about Bathsheba.

Read the text and the Scripture.

Research the rights and responsibilities of a king in ancient times in a Bible dictionary.

- Did David have special rights because he was king?
- Did Bathsheba have the right to refuse David's request?
- Did the king's actions mean consequences for all the people?
- Given that the virility of the king was so important, does this explain or justify taking Bathsheba while she was married? Give a reason for your answer.
- How do most of us react when we discover that our leaders and heroes have "clay feet" like everybody else, and are just as capable of committing sins?

## David (2 Samuel 11:1-5)

David, idolized king of Israel, was thought of as one who could do no wrong, until this incident with Bathsheba. This indiscretion shattered David's power and turned the hopes of his dynasty to dust.

David was the king; he must have thought he could do anything he wanted. He did not know that this incident would be the turning point of his reign and that with this act he would bring ruin on the kingdom and his family for many years to come. The verbs describing what he did are very forceful in action: he spied, he took, he lay—he did it just because he could.

The concept of king developed differently in Israel than in Egypt and in other countries. Kings in Israel were not considered to be gods (as were the pharaohs). God was the supreme ruler in Israel with the king as God's agent. Israel did, however, assume some superstitions about kings from their pagan neighbors, particularly the idea that the king's virility was directly related to the productivity of the people. (If the king was impotent in any way, particularly sexually, the people were in jeopardy.)

### Uriah

Using commentaries and a study Bible, explore the reasons for Uriah's actions. Read the text and the Scripture.

- What rights would Uriah have had if he had discovered his wife got pregnant while he was away at war?
- Why did Uriah disobey the direct orders of the king?
- Why was it so important to Uriah that he avoid going to his home?
- Why, do you think, was Uriah so faithful to the Israelite king and war, when he was himself a foreigner (Hittite)?
- How does the fact that Uriah was a Hittite make David's sin even more glaring?

## Uriah (11:6-27a)

We are not told anything about Bathsheba's feelings about her husband, only that she "made lamentation" for him after his death. We do know that Uriah himself was a loyal, faithful soldier, even though he was a Hittite, not a Hebrew. Uriah is portrayed as altogether innocent in this story: he is the loyal, faithful one who contrasts sharply with the guilty, desperate king.

What else do we know about Uriah?

### Nathan

Look over the text and the Scripture. Invite two group members to reenact the confrontation of Nathan with David, either as the story appears in the Bible or a contemporary version.

- What were the consequences of confronting the truth?
- What risks were taken and by whom?
- When have you had to risk telling the truth? What was the outcome?

## Nathan (11:27b—12:15a)

Nathan confronted the king with his sin at great personal risk. Kings as a rule did not appreciate messengers who presumed to show them the error of their ways. But David was no ordinary king— he confessed his sin at the closing of Nathan's parable when it became clear that David was "the man!"

Many years later Nathan convinced Bathsheba to ask David to declare Solomon his successor. We are not sure of Nathan's motives or of how he felt about Bathsheba. But we do know Nathan was an important figure in the lives of David and Bathsheba.

### The Baby

The baby is the most innocent victim in this drama. Review the text and the Scripture.

- Discuss the import of Bathsheba's news to David that she was pregnant.
- What happens to the baby?
- Is the result just? fair? deserved?
- What does this consequence tell you about God? about the parents?
- How do David and Bathsheba react?

## The Baby (11:15b-23)

Bathsheba shattered the dynasty of David with three little words: "I am pregnant." Nothing was the same after that. Even the child, whose birth was the result of the sin and the reason for David's rash attempts to cover up the sin, did not stand a chance.

### Solomon

Use a Bible dictionary to get an overview of the next man in Bathsheba's life. Review the text and the Scripture.

Look up the name *Solomon* in a Bible dictionary; it is a play on words.

- What does it mean?
- How do the different names for Solomon illuminate the story? the agenda of David and Bathsheba?

### Jesus

Note the presence of Bathsheba in Jesus' genealogy (Matthew 1:6).

- Why, do you think, was she included in the genealogy and without mention of her given name?
- Why do you think Nathan (2 Samuel) and Matthew (Matthew 1) referred to Bathsheba as the wife of Uriah, long after she had become the wife of David?

## Solomon (12:24-25)

Solomon, the second son of David and Bathsheba, was made king over his older brother Adonijah. Solomon promised Adonijah that he would not kill him after his father's death. However when Adonijah asked Bathsheba to request Abishag, David's youngest wife, to be his own wife, Solomon took this as an indirect claim to the throne and had him killed. Bathsheba was again used for the purposes of powerful men.

## Jesus (Matthew 1:1-17)

Bathsheba showed up in the genealogy of Christ given by Matthew in the first chapter of Matthew's Gospel. She is there, herself probably a Hittite like her husband Uriah, along with Tamar (Canaanite), Ruth (Moabitess), and Rahab (Canaanite)—all of whom are also foreign women in Israel. Apparently Bathsheba was considered important enough to be named by Matthew at the most critical moment in history, as an ancestor of the Savior of the world.

# What Else Would We Like to Know About Bathsheba?

*Harsh Consequences*

 Answer and discuss your ideas about Bathsheba's feelings.

## Harsh Consequences

The Scriptures tell us nothing about what Bathsheba felt about the death of her first child. David's grief is described in great detail, but we are not told how Bathsheba felt about this terrible consequence of the sin, except that David consoled her.

Write down how you think Bathsheba felt at the death of her child.

*The Queen*

 Review the text and the Scripture.

Discuss the import of Bathsheba's request to David to name Solomon king.

Discuss the import of Bathsheba's words to Solomon about Adonijah's request.

- It seems that whenever Bathsheba spoke, someone died because the men around her reacted so strongly. What do you think the men who heard her words thought of Bathsheba?
- How could a woman who only speaks three times, whose feelings are never considered important, have this much power?

## The Queen (1 Kings 1:11-21, 28-31; 2 Kings 2:13-25)

Toward the end of her life, Bathsheba was privilege to a very great honor: as the mother of Solomon, the king, she was afforded the greatest respect of any woman in the land. She was the queen mother; it was she who served as First Lady, who sat on the throne next to Solomon—not any woman in the royal harem, wife, or concubine.

Bathsheba played an important role in Solomon's succession as king. It was she who approached David to remind him of his promises to name Solomon as successor; it was she who informed Solomon of the traitorous request of Adonijah regarding Abishag. For a woman who played such a critical part in the story of David, it is only fitting that she receive highest honors at the end of the story.

# How Does What I Know About Bathsheba Affect My Life and Faith?

## Bathsheba, the Woman

 Ask each person to give their reading of today's main story.

- Who do you think is most responsible for what happened?
- What do you think of David? of Nathan? of Bathsheba? of God?
- What difference, if any, did you notice in the way men and women class members responded?
- Do factors such as age, gender, race, socioeconomic status, and occupation affect the way we tend to interpret this story? our faith? If so, how?

## Bathsheba, the Woman

Bathsheba was a wife and "the other woman," even though the latter was probably not from her own initiative.

- How do you think Bathsheba felt about the following men?

Uriah—

David—

Nathan—

*Bathsheba, the Mother*

Discuss how to interpret the story of Bathsheba from the viewpoint of a parent, especially a mother. Answer the questions in the text.

- Has your faith ever conflicted with your responsibility as a parent? If so, how would you describe that experience?

**Bathsheba, the Manipulated and the Manipulator**

Answer and discuss the questions in the text.

Write on a chalkboard or a large piece of paper instances of public figures using their influence to manipulate political or personal circumstances.

- What were the effects of these actions? Who suffered?
- Was there public outrage? Why or why not?
- What were the effects of these actions on the larger community? on the church? on your faith?
- Do we ever forgive public figures for their sins? Why or why not?
- Does God hold public figures more accountable for their sins than other people? Do we?

# Bathsheba, the Mother

- Do you think Bathsheba blamed herself for the death of her first child?

- How do you think she felt about Solomon?

# Bathsheba, the Manipulated and the Manipulator

- Do you think other people blamed Bathsheba for the incident with David?

- Do people still blame her? Who do you hold responsible for what happened?

- When she influenced the succession of Solomon as king, was her "court intrigue" any more appropriate or justifiable than some of the things that had been done to her? Give a reason.

- What does the story of Bathsheba teach us about the results of manipulating others and of being manipulated? about tolerance and forgiveness?

- Bathsheba had a powerful influence over the events of history in the family of God. But she is typically referred to in terms of "Uriah the Hittite," suggesting that she never adhered to the Jewish faith. What difference does that make to the story? to Bathsheba as an influence on your faith?

- What do you think of Bathsheba? How does her story affect your life and faith?

**Worship**

 As a group, write a prayer for the leaders of our own time and for the people of our country. Close with this prayer.

## Chapter Four

# Ruth and Naomi

**CHOOSE FROM AMONG THESE ACTIVITIES TO REFLECT ON HOW RUTH AND NAOMI'S STORY AFFECTS YOUR FAITH.**

*Meet Ruth and Naomi*

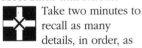 Take two minutes to recall as many details, in order, as you can of the story of Ruth and Naomi. Jot down notes in the space provided. Then take turns reconstructing the story aloud.

Discuss answers to the questions in the text.

## *What Does the Bible Say About Ruth and Naomi?*

### Meet Ruth and Naomi

Pool information about the story of Ruth and Naomi before looking at the text.

● Do any key verses stand out?

● What important memories do you share about the story of Ruth and Naomi?

*Check Your Story*

 Read Ruth in your Bible. Since the book is short, the whole group could read the entire story. Or, form four teams and ask each team to check one chapter.

See how well your memories served you.

### Check Your Story

Jot down notes about what happens in the story.

### What's in a Name?

 Look up the meaning of the characters' names in a Bible dictionary. Either divide the list of names among group members or make a contest out of who can find and record the most definitions and names.

When you have found the meanings of each name, discuss these questions:

● What do the names mean?
● What significance do you think they have for the story?
● Do the names' meanings surprise you? Why?

## What's in a Name?

| Name | Meaning | Relationship to Ruth |
|------|---------|----------------------|
| Elimelech | | |
| Naomi | | |
| Mahlon | | |
| Chilion | | |
| Ruth | friend, companion | self |
| Orpah | | |
| Boaz | | |
| others | | |

## Where's Moab?

 Look at the map showing Moab and the surrounding area. Look also at other maps, either in your study Bibles, Cokesbury's *Bible Teaching Kit*, or Bible atlas.

Review the text as well, then discuss these questions:

- Where is Moab in relation to Israel?
- How far is it from Bethlehem?
- What does it mean that Ruth is from Moab?
- What is the importance of an Israelite family taking residence in Moab and allowing their sons to marry Moabite wives?

## Where's Moab?

Moab is a country to the east of the kingdom of Judah, across the Dead Sea. The Moabites were ancestors to Moab, the son of Lot and the older of Lot's two daughters. Moab was located on the high plateau immediately east of the Dead Sea.

The Israelites tangled with the Moabites regularly from the time of the Exodus to the fall of Jerusalem, around 587 B.C. The Israelites first encountered the Moabites on their way to the Promised Land. Relations between Moabites and Israelites were hostile because of this long, entangled history. At one point, the Israelites could not pass through Moabite lands, and vice-versa. The two nations fought over territory, economics, and religion. Yet they did not entirely separate for many years.

Adapted from *Bible Teacher Kit*, Copyright © 1994 by Abingdon Press.

The two nations were considered to be related peoples because Lot was the nephew of Abraham. The Moabites did not worship the God of the Hebrews. They worshiped many gods, and for this reason the Israelites were forbidden to marry Moabites. However, the sons of Elimelech and Naomi did just that. Apparently the two nations were on friendly enough terms when Elimelech and Naomi migrated there.

Look up the Scriptures mentioned in the text to find out more about Moab. As you have time, discuss these questions:

● What important things did Moses do in Moab?
● What are one or two incidents in Moab-Israelite history that made for bad feelings between the two peoples?

These Scriptures will tell you more about Moab:

◆ Genesis 19:30-38

◆ Deuteronomy 23:2-6

# What Else Would We Like to Know About Ruth and Naomi?

*Widowhood in Bible Days*

 Ask group members to look up the Scriptures in "Widowhood in Bible Days" and to make notes in the spaces provided. A smaller group may use a dictionary or other reference tool about the customs of the biblical era to learn more about marriage and widowhood.

Discuss the material in "Widowhood Today." Compare and contrast then and now.

 ● Discuss the following questions:

● Has the women's movement of our own time in any way affected the way we treat widows? If so, how?
● Is it better to keep women dependent on men and children for their care, like in Bible days, or is it better to expect widows to take care of themselves?
● Who is ultimately responsible for a widow's care?

## Widowhood in Bible Days

First Naomi, then Ruth and Orpah were widowed. Each nation had its own customs about the care of widows and orphans. Israel was one of the only nations whose laws did not allow widows the right to inherit. If a man died before he reached old age, his death was a sin that was blamed on the woman. Widowhood was a disgrace but the prophets and other leaders chided the people strongly for neglecting to care for widows and orphans. The widow was considered to be under the special care of God. The following Scriptures tell us something about Israel's laws and social customs regarding the care for widows.

◆ Leviticus 21:10-15

◆ Deuteronomy 10:12-22

◆ Deuteronomy 14:22-29

◆ Deuteronomy 25:5-10

## Widowhood Today

 Do a role-play activity to compare and contrast widowhood then and now. Ask four persons to take the roles of Ruth, Naomi, a contemporary widow, and a contemporary widower. They will discuss their situations (you decide the ethnicity and economic level of the contemporary figures) while the rest of the group observes silently. When the conversation is over, ask for reflections, observations, insights, and learnings from the observers and answer the questions in the text.

## Gleaning

 Ask group members to use a concordance to locate Scripture references about gleaning. Use Bible dictionaries to find out more about gleaning. After time for research, discuss the following questions.

● What is your impression of the ancient practice of gleaning?
● How do you think Ruth felt?
● Can you think of any contemporary parallels for the practice of gleaning?

# Widowhood Today

Describe how you think widows are treated in your own culture:

● Do you think ethnic background (European American, African American, Asian American, Hispanic American, Native American, and so on) makes a difference in the way widows are treated? If so, how?

# Gleaning

Gleaning is the practice of gathering what has been dropped or left on the vine or in the field after a harvest. Technically, gleaners were also allowed to harvest what was left standing in the corners of the field. Hebrew law said an owner could not clean up his own field, vineyard, or orchard, so that the widow, the orphan, and alien resident could be fed.

### How Did Ruth and Naomi Survive?

Review Ruth Chapters 2–3. Research these chapters in a Bible commentary. Using the space provided, note findings about the dangers and opportunities Ruth and Naomi faced.

- What are some of the dangers? opportunities?
- What did the commentary suggest about the dangers? about the opportunities?
- What new insights to the women's situation did you gain?
- What values and principles emerged in your assessment of the way Ruth and Naomi handled their situation?

Review the text and answer the questions.

## Ruth and Naomi: Partners in Survival

- Chapters 2 and 3 of the Book of Ruth reveal how Naomi and Ruth planned for their survival. They faced several dangers and challenges. Which ones can you identify?

- Fortunately, Boaz was an honorable man and contributed in his own way to their well-being. What help did Boaz provide?

- What do you think of Naomi's plan for Ruth with Boaz? Do you agree with her method for giving him the idea of marrying Ruth?

# How Does What I Know About Ruth and Naomi Affect My Life and Faith?

## Evaluate Changing Relationships

 Examine the changes in Ruth and Naomi's relationships with each other and with the other persons they encountered and left behind. Talk briefly about those changes, then discuss the following questions:

- How did Ruth and Naomi's relationship change?
- Have you had to make any of the same kind of changes in your relationships? If so, did you feel comfortable telling others about the circumstance and explaining the reasons?
- How do you feel about Orpah? Why do you think she made the decision she did? What would you have done in her situation?

## Relationships

As Ruth and Naomi's circumstances changed, so did their relationships. They met new people, entered into new relationships, and dealt with each other in ways that their relocation to Bethlehem demanded.

Orpah is sometimes portrayed as the villain of the story, the one who abandoned her mother-in-law and went back home. In fact, Orpah did what was expected of her. She went back to care for her own mother, to worship her own gods, and to live as a citizen of her community. The story does not say if Ruth left behind a mother or a family. The radical action here is Ruth's, not Orpah's. Orpah did the right thing; Ruth did the extraordinary thing.

Scan the biblical text again, looking for the obvious and not-so-obvious ways God was at work on behalf of the story's participants.

Use commentaries to help understand the Jewish laws that called persons to acts of charity and mercy. Use the space provided for notes and reflections.

When the research is done, discuss in general your findings.

● In what ways is God's interaction expected? unexpected?
● What are some of the social and legal requirements that called for personal charity and mercy?
● Do these requirements make sense today? Why or why not?
● Are there similar ways in which you find God at work in your life?
● Did anything in Ruth or Naomi's experience trigger a realization of the work of God in your life? What?

## Where Is God in the Story?

A foundation of the story is not only the human and loving loyalty of one woman for another, but also their loyalty to God and God's loyalty to the people. Many of the Scripture references mention God's involvement in this poignant drama. Some of these references are implied; that is, Israel had certain godly laws that mandated them to act in the loving ways God commanded. Others are more obvious; God is mentioned specifically.

● How many references to God, both implied and direct, can you find?

*Worship*

 Talk or write about the session as a whole and reflect on what you have experienced today. Use the questions in the text to help you summarize. Close with a brief prayer.

## In Closing

● How did you personally experience this session?

● What insights or new learnings did you gain?

● What assumptions or beliefs were challenged?

● What does this story say about God?

● How does this story affect your faith?

## Chapter Five

# Elizabeth

### Who is Elizabeth?

 Read Luke 1:5-80. To save time, assign various verses to class members.

● Why do you think Zechariah was told about the impending birth in this instance instead of Elizabeth, but Mary was told directly (as was Hannah, the wife of Manoah, and Sarah)?

● Why was Zechariah struck mute?

● How does the praise song of Zechariah (Luke 1:68-79) differ from Mary's Magnificat (Luke 1:46-55)?

### Activity: Surprises

 Distribute paper and pens. Ask the class members to write down the biggest surprise of their life. Invite those who are willing to share their surprises with the class. Discuss these questions with each surprise:

● Was the surprise good or bad?

# What Does the Bible Say About Elizabeth?

## Who is Elizabeth? Daughter, Wife, Mother, Sister

Most of us know very little about Elizabeth, save that she was the mother of John the Baptist. But the Scriptures offer a glimpse of a life rich in tradition, faith, and miracle. Elizabeth lived a blameless life, according to the commandments, as befitted the wife of a priest.

- How did you react?
- Do you like surprises?
- Did the surprise have a lasting effect on your life?
- How did you deal with this surprise?

*Daughter of Aaron*

 Form four groups and assign one of the following passages to each group. Have them read about Aaron, his priestly duties, and the importance and responsibilities of the Levitic line.

♦ Exodus 4:10-17

♦ Leviticus 6:8—7:38

♦ Leviticus 16

♦ Deuteronomy 18

Refer to the Chart of the Levitical Offerings for a more complete understanding of the priestly duties.

Ask each group to consider these questions:
- Why was the purity of the priest so important?
- What effect do you think this expectation had on Elizabeth's life?

## Daughter of Aaron

A simple phrase in the story of Elizabeth is packed full of meaning: "His wife was a descendant of Aaron." Skimming over these simple words is easy, unless we think about what they mean. Aaron was the brother of Moses, the one chosen to speak for Moses when he went before Pharoah because Moses had a tendency to stutter. Aaron was the first Levite, a priest whose responsibilities included teaching God's decrees, offering prescribed sacrifices, and officiating at services of atonement. He established the house of Aaron; those born as descendants of Aaron were destined for priesthood.

Elizabeth, whose own lineage was in the house of Aaron, married a priest. Her whole life was devoted to the Temple: leading, serving, and ministering had been her honorable duty all her life, first with her father, and now with Zechariah, her husband. But there was a problem. She could not seem to accomplish the one duty which was the most important of all: she was unable to give Zechariah a child.

But that problem was about to change.

*The Barren One*

 Ask class members to look up other stories of special children born to women supposedly barren. Use a commentary to bring further light to the references.

♦ Sarah:
Genesis 17:15-19
Genesis 21:1-7

♦ Rebekah:
Genesis 25:21-27

♦ Rachel:
Genesis 29:31; 30:1-2, 22-24
Genesis 35:16-19

# *What Else Would We Like to Know About Elizabeth?*

## The Barren One

A woman's most critical duty was to produce an heir in the house of her husband. Even if the husband was sterile, failure to produce an heir was always considered to be the fault of the woman.

Write down what you think Elizabeth must have felt about her barren state as a younger woman.

- ♦ Wife of Manoah:
  Judges 13:2-25

- ♦ Hannah:
  1 Samuel 1:1-11, 19-20

- ● How is the story of Elizabeth different from these
  other birth stories? How is
  it similar?
- ● Samson was to be a
  Nazirite, just like John the
  Baptist, but he broke his
  vows and was unfaithful.
- ● How was John's life different from Samson's,
  despite similar beginnings?

Discuss responses to
the writing activity
in the text.

Write down what you think Elizabeth felt about her barren state as an older, post-menopausal woman.

### *The Clergy Wife*

Research Levites and
the Levitical tradition
and the role of
wives in a Bible dictionary.
Ask the class to read carefully Elizabeth's duties, which
are provided in Luke 1:6,
and to postulate what other
duties or expectations might
be included.

## The Clergy Wife
Elizabeth's responsibility was much larger than simply the continuance of Zechariah's line. He was a priest, and the spiritual health of the community depended upon the continuance of the house of Aaron. If Zechariah failed to have an heir, some other member of the house of Aaron would have to step in.

- How is the role of clergy spouse similar and/or different today?
- Do you think the fact that she was a public figure influenced her decision to go into seclusion when she got pregnant?

Review answers to the questions in the text.

- Think about your own pastor and his or her family. Do you think most Christians prefer to have a pastor with a spouse and children? Give a reason for your answer.

- Is this expectation appropriate? Why or why not?

- What kind of expectations does your congregation have for your pastor and his or her spouse and/or children? Are these expectations appropriate?

- How do you think Elizabeth felt about the public pressure added to her personal shame over her childless state? (see Luke 1:24-25)

Review the text and write down your ideas about Elizabeth's pregnancy.

Elizabeth was resigned to her fate. She understood that motherhood was not to be part of her life. She was reconciled. She lived a full, busy, righteous life, and she was probably looking forward to the golden retirement years with Zechariah.

Then one day her world turned upside down. Her priest husband came home completely mute for no apparent reason. How ironic that this priest, whose ancestor Aaron was chosen to speak for Moses because of his able tongue, could not even tell his wife the news of her pregnancy and the special child she would carry. If she were literate, perhaps he was able to write her a note, but even so, how bewildered she must have been, especially when it became clearly evident that she was indeed pregnant.

For some reason Elizabeth decided to hide herself. Perhaps she could not endure the gentle ribbing from the congregation. Perhaps Zechariah wanted her at home—it was enough for him to deal with his disability and still perform his duties. Perhaps Elizabeth was afraid because she knew her age put her at high risk for a miscarriage, and if it turned out there would be no child after all, her disgrace would have been unendurable.

Write down how you think Elizabeth felt about her pregnancy.

### The Visitor

 A wonderful description of the relationship between Mary and Elizabeth is offered by Renita Weems in her book *Just a Sister Away.* The chapter is called "Unbegrudged Blessings." Weem's describes

## The Visitor

Mary sought the counsel of her elder cousin, who was also mysteriously and frighteningly pregnant. There was nobody else Mary could talk to—she hoped Elizabeth would understand. Elizabeth understood very well, especially how Mary's visit might have been for both women, and that they could be a unique source of support for each other that neither woman could find any other place. If you can get a copy of this book, this chapter would highlight the relationship in a way the class has probably never heard before.

Discuss the reflection statement in the text.

### *Who Is This Special Child?*

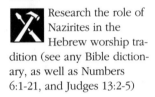 Research the role of Nazirites in the Hebrew worship tradition (see any Bible dictionary, as well as Numbers 6:1-21, and Judges 13:2-5)

- Why was it important that John the Baptist be a Nazirite, like Samson and Samuel before him?
- Why do you think John the Baptist was to be a Nazirite, but not Jesus? (See Matthew 9:14-17.)

Ask group members to look at these Scriptures for the life of John the Baptist and his relationship with Jesus:

♦ Matthew 3:1-17

♦ Luke 3:1-22

♦ John 1:19-34

when her own child leaped for joy in her womb at Mary's greeting.

Write down how you would feel (or perhaps have felt) in an intimate encounter with the Savior of the world.

## Who Is This Special Child?

Elizabeth's child was to be the herald, the proclaimer, the opening act for God's mightiest miracle in the history of humankind. God was about to perform a miracle never before seen in history: the one God would enter the world as a human baby. John's destiny was to be the first to tell the world about the Savior. Zechariah was given instructions about how John was to live: he was to be a Nazirite; that is, a child consecrated or set aside for Temple service who was never to cut his hair or imbibe strong drink. John was to be different, to be set apart.

# How Does What I Know About Elizabeth Affect My Life and Faith?

*Unanswered Prayer*

 Research as many instances as you can of Bible figures who did not get their prayers answered in the way they expected (Job, Jonah, Jesus). This could be a springboard for a discussion on how to endure with faith when you must face disappointment and pain.

 If participants are willing, ask them to answer and discuss the writing assignment and questions in the text.

## Unanswered Prayer

Elizabeth prayed for many years to have a child, but as she grew older she had to accept that it would not happen.

Write down some instances in your own life when you have felt barren or bereft and as if your most cherished prayers would not be answered.

• Did you discover later that your prayer had been answered, perhaps in a way you did not expect?

• What was that experience like?

*Two Women; Two Sisters*

 For women and men, sometimes the way we deal with other people of our gender is with competition and suspicion.

Review Luke 1:39-56 concerning the relationship between Elizabeth and Mary. Ask class members to write responses to the activity in the text.

- How would you summarize their relationship?
- What kind of risks does it take to develop meaningful friendships with people of your gender?
- What are the benefits of taking such risks?

## Two Women; Two Sisters

Mary, a young girl, sought out Elizabeth, her elder. Mary expected to show deference to Elizabeth, as an elder cousin, but Elizabeth loudly praised Mary as "the mother of my Lord." They became more than cousins at that point; they were united as sisters.

Write down reasons these two women might have been rivals.

Write down reasons for these two women to be friends.

## *The Beginning*

 Work on the questions in the text. Discuss any new insights.

## The Beginning

- What surprises have come to you in your own life that changed your life forever?

- How has God brought you out when you felt barren?

- Have you ever felt that you were called to do something unique and special for God? If so, how would you describe that experience? How did you feel about it?

## *Worship*

 Read together the quote from Isaiah found in Luke 3:4-6. Close with prayer.

- What can Elizabeth teach you (and others) about facing an uncertain future?

# Mary

## What Does the Bible Say About Mary?

*Mary of History;
Mary of Faith*

 Ask group members to talk about what they know about Mary. Write down the answers on a chalkboard or poster paper.

### Mary of History; Mary of Faith

Write down everything you know about Mary, mother of Jesus.

*Just the Facts*

 Assign each participant one of the Bible passages to read. If the class is large, divide the class into small groups, and assign the passages to groups.

Use these questions as discussion starters:

● Did you discover any new information you did not already know about Mary? If so, what?
● Are there any facts about Mary you thought were in the Bible, but in fact are not? If so, what?
● Why do you think Mary has been such a pivotal figure in the life of the church?
● What is it about Mary and the life she lived that means the most to you?

Discuss facts about Mary gleaned from the passages.

# Just the Facts

Write down all the facts you can glean from your assigned Bible reading about Mary.

◆ Matthew 1—2
◆ Luke 1—2
◆ John 2:1-12
◆ Matthew 12:46-50
◆ John 19:25-27

*From Bible Scholarship*

 Discuss the social implications for Mary and her family caused by her pregnancy.

Talk about being chosen by God: is it a blessing or a burden or both?

Ask the class to discuss what sacrifices have been required of them for the honor of being chosen and blessed by God.

## What Do We Know About Mary From Bible Scholarship?

We know some facts about Mary which are not in the Bible, but which can be assumed from what we know about first century Jewish culture or are reported in noncanonical texts from that era.

◆ Mary was probably between 12 and 14 years old when she wed Joseph.

◆ Joseph was much older than Mary.

◆ First century Jews practiced a two-step matrimonial procedure: 1) a formal exchange of consent before witnesses (betrothal) and 2) subsequent taking of the bride into the groom's family home. The interlude between the two steps could be as much as a year. Mary and Joseph were in between the steps, which means that they were legally married, but she was still living in her parents' home. Sometimes betrothed couples were allowed to be alone together (as Mary and Joseph were on the long journey to Bethlehem), depending upon the traditions of a particular region. But Matthew and Luke are very clear on one point: Mary was a virgin.

◆ Adultery was a capital crime, punishable by death (usually by stoning). Joseph had the right to demand that Mary be tried as a criminal, to be put to death. He is referred to as an "upright man" because he planned to divorce her quietly. The public shame and scorn would be terrible for her when her pregnancy became apparent, but she would not die for the "crime."

## The Mothering of God

Mary must have experienced considerable turmoil in the events in the life of her first-born son. She was widowed young, which meant that it was Jesus' responsibility to care for her, but he renounced his mother and family no fewer than three times in the Gospels.

Investigate those instances.

◆ Luke 2:41-51

◆ Matthew 12:46-50 (Mark 3:31-35; Luke 8:19-21)

◆ John 7:1-9

*The Mothering of God*

 Read and discuss the Scripture passages.

● Why did Mary "treasure all these things in her heart" after she had been so panicked about Jesus?
● What do you think Mary felt after Jesus' statements and actions?
● How do you think she explained her son's actions to her family, friends, and neighbors?
● Where do you see instances of her courage and wisdom?

Make three columns on the board. Title them "Securities," "Risks," and "Solutions." List the securities in Mary's life, events that put these securities at risk, and some of the solutions she devised to solve the problem.

For example:
*Securities*: Childhood home/Virgin status
*Risks*: The angel's news of her pregnancy
*Solutions*: She asked the angel for explanations; she consulted with Elizabeth; she trusted God for the rest

Review the Scripture references.

Mary has received bad press for appearing to be ignorant of the purposes of God in the life of Jesus, but in fact Mary understood him very well. She knew he had a vision for a new kind of family—not based on the secure, closed family relational units we struggle to maintain for our children, but upon love for God and for our neighbors that goes far and beyond blood relationships. Notice her courage and strength as she questions the angel, coaxes Jesus into a miracle, and faces the Crucifixion.

◆ Luke 1:26-37

◆ John 2:1-11

◆ John 19:16-27

# What Else Would We Like to Know About Mary?

## Mary—Love for Protestants

 Put together a list of what you think Catholics believe about Mary then look at the text.

- Which beliefs are accurate and which are stereotypes?
- What is your belief about Mary and her role in the Christian faith?
- Is she, can she be, or should she be an intercessor between persons and God? Give a reason for your answer.
- How does her role and example affect your understanding of Jesus and his ministry?

## Mary—Love for Protestants

Christians have been curious about and reverent of Mary from the first days of the early church. Mary has been portrayed as about as close to God as any earthly person could get; after all, she did carry the Son of God in her womb for nine months. But the piety for Mary that has developed over the years goes far beyond the physical fact of her pregnancy. Mary is somehow more approachable, more reachable than any other figure close to Christ. As one described as the mother of God, she seems to be mother of us all—a mother who can tell us the real story of God and Christ, just as our own mothers told us the first truths about the world.

As the church developed through the years, the laity and clergy became more and more disconnected. Sacraments at one time were reserved only for clergy; worship and Scripture (if accessible at all) was in a language common folk did not understand. Religion for many became mysterious, even magical.

The people needed to be reconnected in an intimate relationship with God; Mary was the perfect choice as an intermediary, someone who could connect them to God again. Reverence for Mary slowly developed into worship of Mary. You could touch Mary and be assured of nurture and care; the people were afraid to think of Jesus or God in such intimate terms. Prayer through Mary became commonplace.

In 1854 Pope Pius IX declared the doctrine of Immaculate Conception: the conception of Mary without sin, which elevated Mary's status even higher. During the Protestant Reformation, worship of Mary (among other things) became highly suspect as the church divided. Protestants are still uneasy with Mariology (worship and reverence of Mary) and of the notion that Christians need any mediator standing between ourselves and God when we pray.

*Reclaiming the Treasure*

 Review the text, then offer suggestions for ways United Methodists can reclaim Mary as a treasure for our faith.

Name other women, either in the Bible or from your experience, who are foundational for the church.

● What is her contribution?
● What has that meant to you and your faith?

## Reclaiming the Treasure

When the Protestant church stepped away from worshiping Mary, we lost almost all feminine symbols: Mary, female saints, and nuns. Christian symbols became largely male in Protestant faiths: God, Jesus, the Holy Spirit, church leaders, pastors—all were male. Yet women have historically provided a foundation of support without which the church could never have been the church. (See for example, Luke 8:1-3 and Acts 1:14.)

Mary is a treasure for all Christians, Protestants included. She offers hope to all Christians; in Mary we can see that no matter how we suffer, no matter how our lives turn out, there is still hope; there is always faith.

# How Does What I Know About Mary Affect My Life and Faith?

## *How It Really Was...*

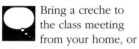 Bring a creche to the class meeting from your home, or take time in the class to examine a nativity scene in the church. Look at (or picture in your mind) the nativity scene.

● How close do you think our depictions of the birth are to how it really was?

● As you think about childbirth, how do you envision the suitability of a stable or a cave? the fact that Mary was attended only by her husband with no medical help or implements?

● Is Mary serene and happy? How do you think she really feels?

● Why is it so important for us to lay out the figurines every Advent season? What does this scene mean for Christians?

● Does it trouble you to talk about the realities of the birth, as opposed to the sentiments we have placed on the event? Give a reason for your answer.

## How It Really Was...

Have you noticed that as the years roll by, the birth story of Christ becomes more sterile, more soft, even more cute? Since we are so remote from the primitive conditions of early Palestine, it is hard to imagine what that birth was really like.

You can imagine the shock and horror experienced by Mary's parents and Joseph when they discovered she was pregnant. Almost as soon as she received the news, Mary made a trip to visit her cousin Elizabeth, perhaps to provide herself some time to think for awhile. She returned home as Elizabeth was about to give birth to John. But before she was taken into Joseph's home as his wife, Joseph was called away for a census in Bethlehem. Mary, nine months pregnant, and very close to delivery, went with him.

*Mother of God...for Us*

Protestants do not pray to Mary to intercede for us. But maybe our knowledge of Mary can change the way we pray. Read aloud the Magnificat (Luke 1:46-55), then write a prayer with Mary's vision for humankind in mind.

- What assumptions did you have about Mary before this session?
- How have you changed as a result of today's study?

*Worship*

Close with a reading of the written prayer.

## Mother of God...for Us

Mary has been revered and reviled, worshiped and ignored, loved and misunderstood from the day Gabriel dropped in for a visit with startling news.

- How do you feel about Mary? Write down what Mary means to you or what you would like for her to mean to you.

## Chapter Seven

# The Woman Caught in Adultery

**CHOOSE FROM AMONG THESE ACTIVITIES TO REFLECT ON HOW THE WOMAN'S STORY AFFECTS YOUR FAITH.**

*How It Might Have Been*

 Read John 7:53— 8:11 aloud. Discuss first impressions of the story.

Speculate on what Jesus may have been writing in the dirt. No one really knows, but some of the reasons might include:

● Jesus was angry, so he was "counting to ten" to contain or hide his feelings.
● He was buying time so he could make the right decision.
● There is a rabbinic tradition in which the rabbi would draw in the ground while his students would ponder a question.
● Raymond Brown, in his *Anchor Bible* commentary on John (pages 333-334), offers these traditional suggestions:
a) Jesus wrote the sins of the accusers
b) Jesus emulated Roman judges who wrote down a sentence before reading it aloud.

# What Does the Bible Say About the Woman Caught in Adultery?

## How it Might Have Been

It was a quiet, peaceful morning in the women's court of the Temple. Jesus sat there teaching as usual. He taught in the women's court because he wanted the women to hear what he had to say and they were not allowed in any other part of the Temple. Into this idyllic setting roared a crowd of screaming, angry men, dragging a bedraggled woman. They pushed her in front of Jesus, told him they caught her in the very act of adultery, and asked him what he had to say. They already had the stones in their hands; they were ready to execute the death penalty against her. The crowd of scribes and Pharisees hounded Jesus, asking him over and over again, "Well, Teacher, what do you have to say?"

Jesus wrote in the dirt.

The men pressed on, demanding his answer. They could not wait for him to fall into their trap. They had been salivating for days, waiting for the chance to condemn him, to catch him saying something they could point to so they could

c) He was acting out Jeremiah 17:13.

d) He wrote the words of Exodus 23:1*b*.

e) Jesus was taking time to think, to gauge his emotions.

Look up the two references mentioned by Brown. Discuss what the group thinks Jesus was writing in the dirt, and then discuss if this question is irrelevant.

bring him before the authorities. Surely the plan would not fail this time. They pushed him further, "Teacher! What do you have to say?"

Jesus was still writing in the dirt.

Then he straightened up, looked the mob in the eye and said, quietly and simply, words that rocked the universe: "Let anyone among you who is without sin be the first to throw a stone at her."

Absolute silence. His words hung heavy in the air. Nobody said anything because there was nothing to say. One by one, the men went quietly away, cursing Jesus under their breath.

Jesus wrote in the dirt.

Then he looked up, saw this frightened, bedraggled woman before him, and asked her very gently, "Where are they? Has no one condemned you?" "No one, sir." "Neither do I condemn you. Go...and do not sin again."

That is the story, simple and profound as it is. No more; no less—but this story has confounded Christians through the ages.

***What the Bible Doesn't Say***

Research how Jesus treated women in his lifetime. Look up the term *woman* in a concordance, and read how it is used in stories about Jesus. Then look up the following passages:

◆ Mark 5:24-34

◆ Mark 7:24-30

◆ John 4:1-30

● How do you think Jesus felt about women?
● Was the way he treated women considered radical, even dangerous by some? Why?

Discuss answers to the questions in the text.

# What the Bible Doesn't Say

Many assumptions and interpretations have been added to this story by tradition, mostly because the story, as it is, makes us uncomfortable. Here is a list of what the Bible does not say in this story:

◆ if she were a hardened sinner or prostitute;
◆ if she were willing; she might in fact have been raped or assaulted;
◆ that her act was not a sin;
◆ who she was (some have assumed she was Mary Magdalene, but clearly she was not);
◆ what happened to her afterward;
◆ what happened to her partner or who he was;
◆ how the woman felt or if she were sorry for her sin.

● What assumptions did you make about this story before you read it?

● Were you surprised by anything on this list of what the Bible does not say?

Write down who you think the woman might have been, what she might have felt, and what might have happened to her after she encountered Jesus.

# What Else Would We Like to Know About the Woman Caught in Adultery?

### *Adultery*

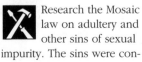 Research the Mosaic law on adultery and other sins of sexual impurity. The sins were considered much bigger than the individuals involved; the entire nation and people of Israel were threatened when this kind of sin was committed. Read Leviticus 18.

- Why, do you think, were these sins such a big deal in Israel?
- What kind of threat did these sins pose to the nation?

Read Leviticus 20:10 and Deuteronomy 22:22-30.

- According to the law, who in this story should die for the crime of adultery?
- Where is this woman's partner?
- What might have happened to him?

## Adultery

It is difficult for us to understand why the crowd was so angry with this woman. Adultery is a big sin with us too, but we do not lawfully execute people for it. Why were these men so angry with her?

Adultery was considered a violation of property rights. A wife was a man's property and she could be put to death for becoming "damaged goods." A man who committed adultery with a married or betrothed woman could also be put to death—but not if the woman was not married—because he had violated another man's property. In that case, he had to marry the woman, never to divorce.

Sexual sins defiled the land under the Jewish law. Adultery was a very serious thing. That is why it required two witnesses, other than the husband. The fact that she was caught in the act of intercourse justified the actions of the crowd. The woman's guilt is not in question; there were plenty of witnesses; she could now be put to death.

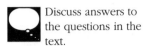 Discuss answers to the questions in the text.

- What are your own attitudes about people who commit adultery? What should happen to them?

- Do you agree that the woman's sin was real?

- If someone in your church were caught like this, how would your church respond? How would you respond?

### *The Trap*

 This story is not the only one about Jewish authorities trying to trap Jesus. Look up John 7:25-31, the prelude to this story, and John 10:31-39; 11:55-57 (plots against Jesus); and 12:9-11 (let's just kill off Lazarus, too).

● What portrait emerges of the authorities' desires for Jesus?
● What does this picture have to do with the woman?

 Look up *stoning* in a Bible dictionary. After the first century, the Pharisees generally shifted to strangulation as the punishment of choice.

Read Acts 6:8-15; 7:54-69 then Acts 14:19.

● What were the circumstances under which these persons, including the woman, were stoned?
● What do you think of this practice?
● Did Stephen, Paul, and the woman caught in adultery put the community in jeopardy? If so, how?
● Do you think stoning is an appropriate punishment for a criminal who puts the community at danger?
● What might be a modern equivalent to stoning today?

Discuss the answers to the questions in the text.

### The Trap

The Romans took away the right of the Sanhedrin (Jewish court) to execute people around 30 A.D., which is about the date this incident occurred. However, Jewish law (Mosaic law) clearly stated that they had every right, and even a responsibility to the community, to execute this woman. If Jesus said he condemned the woman, he would be violating his own religious law; if he said he did not condemn her, he would be violating the Roman decree. He would be in trouble either way.

● Why do you think the scribes and Pharisees wanted to trap Jesus?

● What do you think Jesus had done to make the scribes and Pharisees so angry?

## The Counter-Trap

Look up *Pharisee, scribe,* and *Sadducee* in a Bible dictionary. Discuss the fact that these Jewish authorities (sort of like our pastors and seminary professors) were the professional people who upheld the law and called the people to repentance.

- How do these religious authorities appear in the various Scripture readings? Do you think all Pharisees were this way? Why or why not?
- Why was Jesus so irritated with the Pharisees on this occasion and many others?
- Do we as Christian church members identify more with the Pharisees or the sinful woman? How?
- Why do you think the Pharisees felt threatened by Jesus?
- What moral responsibility did the Pharisees have to the community?

## The Counter-Trap

Jesus trapped the scribes and Pharisees in their own accusation. While what they were doing might have been legally right according to the law of Moses, it was not morally right. These men were using the woman to set a trap for Jesus. They were scapegoating her. The motives of the accusers caused Jesus to react (or not react) the way he did. They evidently did not care about this woman at all, except as an instrument they could use to trap Jesus. Perhaps that is why her partner in adultery is conspicuously absent.

How did Jesus trap the Pharisees and thwart their plan to trap him? Jesus put a new twist to an old law. Read Deuteronomy 17:6-7. The old law says that the Pharisees had every right to do what they were doing.

- How did Jesus use this law against the Pharisees?
- Why do you think Jesus twisted the situation around so that the Pharisees ended up condemning themselves instead of the woman?
- Did Jesus excuse what she did?

Discuss your answers to the questions in the text.

- What do you think Jesus thought of the scheme?

- How do you think Jesus felt about this woman?

- Why do you think Jesus did not condemn the woman when she was so clearly a sinner?

# How Does What I Know About the Woman Caught in Adultery Affect My Life and Faith?

## *To Condemn, Condone, or Forgive*

 Jot down, then review your answers to the questions in the text.

- What does this story teach about repentance? about condemnation? about forgiveness?
- Have you ever needed the benefit of the doubt and been denied it? received it? How did it feel? What kind of impact did that experience (or experiences) make on your faith?

## To Condemn, Condone, or Forgive

It is important to note that Jesus did not offer forgiveness to the woman. He did not condemn or condone her. What he offered was a new start, a chance to redeem herself. He gave her a choice: choose life or death.

- Why do you think Jesus let her go?

- It might be easier for us if Jesus clearly condemned her, then clearly forgave her. It would make more sense to us. As it is, we do not even know if she was sorry for her sin. Is it possible to forgive people who have not said they were sorry for their sin?

With this more complete view of Jesus' relationship with others, write an ending to the story of the woman caught in adultery. Ask a volunteer to describe his or her version of the end of the story.

Talk about forgiveness. Jesus certainly implied forgiveness by refusing to accuse and by encouraging the woman to go and not sin again. But we all do sin again.

● What does this story suggest about the availability and source of forgiveness? about the nature of human beings? about personal and corporate responsibility as children of God?

### Worship

 Summarize your learnings from the session and close with prayer.

● The scribes and Pharisees ended up condemning themselves because they knew they were not without sin. In what ways do we condemn ourselves?

● Immediately following this story, Jesus says, "I am the light of the world. Whoever follows me will never walk in darkness but will have the light of life" (John 8:12). How is this good news in your life?